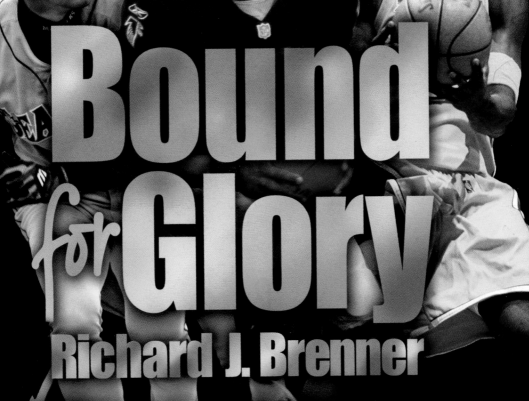

Bound for Glory

Richard J. Brenner

An East End Publishing Book • Syosset, NY

Author's Note The players in this book are gifted athletes, but they all had to work hard and overcome obstacles in order to achieve their dreams. Even a superstar like Kobe Bryant has had to face some very tough times, but instead of letting obstacles stand in his way, he goads himself into overcoming them. "Everything negative, whether it's pressure or challenges, I see as an opportunity for me to rise."

You can become a superstar too, if you want to work for it. There are lots of areas for you to consider besides athletics. You could help clean up the environment or work for world peace; you could become a musician, a teacher, a doctor, a human rights activist or a writer. Superstar ecologists and caregivers are probably more important than superstar athletes.

Mr. Brenner, America's best-selling sportswriter, has written dozens of exciting sports books, including: KURT WARNER*PEYTON MANNING, a dual biography, and a series of easy-to-read, photo-filled biographies of Brett Favre, Derek Jeter, Mark McGwire, Sammy Sosa and Kobe Bryant.

For complete details on how to order these and other exciting sports books, please see back page.

Mr. Brenner is also available to speak at schools. For details, contact East End Publishing, Ltd., 54 Alexander Dr., Syosset, NY 11791, call (516) 364-6383 or e-mail rbrenne2@optonline.net.

Design and layout: *Jeannette Jacobs*
Copy editor: *Mike Simon*
Proofreader: *John Douglas*

All the photographs of Ichiro Suzuki were supplied by SportsChrome; **Tom DiPace** took the one on page 3, all the others, including the cover photo were taken by **Michael Zito**, as were the photos on pages 22 and 25. Sports Chrome also supplied the following photographs (photographer's names are in parenthesis): All the interior photos of Alfonso Soriano (**Rob Tringali**); page 28 (**Bongarts**). **Steven Murphy** of Sports Picture Network took the cover photograph of Michael Vick, and the one on page 19. All the other photographs were supplied by Icon Sports Media, as per the following: page 15 (**Chris Livingston**), page 16 (**Dale Zanine**); the cover photo of Kobe Bryant and page 21 (**John McDonough/SI**); pages 27 and 31 (**Ray Stubblebine**); the cover photo of Alfonso Soriano (**John Cordes**), the cover photo of Yao Ming (**A.J. Mast**).

ISBN: 0-943403-64-2

Published by EAST END PUBLISHING, LTD.
54 Alexander Dr.
Syosset, NY 11791
Printed in the United States of America.

This book is dedicated to all the people of the earth: May you always play in peace and happiness, walk in beauty, and work to build communities that are free from hate, fear, and bigotry of every type.

This book is also dedicated to my parents, whose love lives on in my memory, and to Jerry Geller, Marvin Gluckman and Barry Silverstein, old friends who are gone but still warmly remembered.

With great appreciation to everybody whose time and talents have contributed so much to this book, including, Jeannette Jacobs, John Douglas, Randy Lawrence, Frances Gilbert and Mike Simon.

Thanks are also due, as usual, to all my friends at Scholastic Book Fairs, most especially Alan Boyko and Janet Speakman.

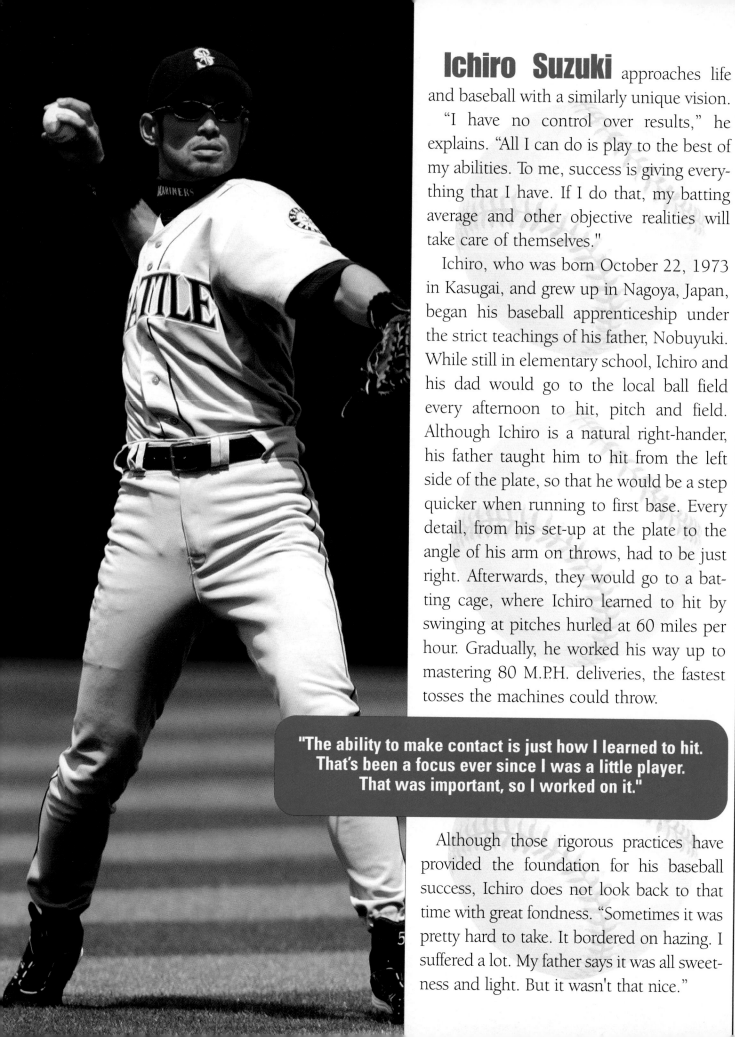

Ichiro Suzuki approaches life and baseball with a similarly unique vision.

"I have no control over results," he explains. "All I can do is play to the best of my abilities. To me, success is giving everything that I have. If I do that, my batting average and other objective realities will take care of themselves."

Ichiro, who was born October 22, 1973 in Kasugai, and grew up in Nagoya, Japan, began his baseball apprenticeship under the strict teachings of his father, Nobuyuki. While still in elementary school, Ichiro and his dad would go to the local ball field every afternoon to hit, pitch and field. Although Ichiro is a natural right-hander, his father taught him to hit from the left side of the plate, so that he would be a step quicker when running to first base. Every detail, from his set-up at the plate to the angle of his arm on throws, had to be just right. Afterwards, they would go to a batting cage, where Ichiro learned to hit by swinging at pitches hurled at 60 miles per hour. Gradually, he worked his way up to mastering 80 M.P.H. deliveries, the fastest tosses the machines could throw.

> "The ability to make contact is just how I learned to hit. That's been a focus ever since I was a little player. That was important, so I worked on it."

Although those rigorous practices have provided the foundation for his baseball success, Ichiro does not look back to that time with great fondness. "Sometimes it was pretty hard to take. It bordered on hazing. I suffered a lot. My father says it was all sweetness and light. But it wasn't that nice."

Following a spectacular high school career, Ichiro was drafted in 1991 by the Orix Blue Wave, and spent the following two seasons playing for their minor league team in the Western League. Although the Orix manager had directed him to alter his hitting style, Ichiro defied Japanese custom, and insisted on maintaining his individual approach at the plate. "If something works," he explained, "there's no need to change it."

He's very intelligent," former teammate David Bell said. "As far as understanding his game and his swing and what he has to do, he's at another level."

Two years later, Ichiro, who had finished the 1993 season as the Western League's batting champion and MVP, was promoted to the Japanese big leagues and immediately began carving out a legendary career. In his first campaign with the Blue Wave, the 20-year-old Ichiro led the Pacific League in batting with a .385 average, won a Gold Glove for his fielding abilities and was named the 1994 MVP.

It was the first of seven consecutive batting titles and Gold Gloves for Ichiro, who also went on to claim two more MVP awards, while leading the Blue Wave to a pair of Western League pennants and a Japan Series win in 1996 over the Yomiuri Giants, the most famous and successful team in the country.

"He's just one of those players who has a different gear when he needs it," said Chris Donnels, a former major league infielder, who also played for the Blue Wave from 1997-1999. "It's something that you can't teach, and very few guys have it."

Despite the fact that he had clearly established himself as the greatest player in Japan, Ichiro was determined to raise the bar and test himself against the competition in the American Major Leagues. "It was time to move up," he explained in November 2000, after he'd signed a three-year contract to play for the Seattle Mariners. "I had heard that in the United States, the level of baseball was the highest in the world. As an athlete, you have to compete against the world's best."

When spring training began, many people doubted that Ichiro, the first Japanese everyday position player in the majors, would be able to hit big-league pitchers, despite a ringing endorsement

Ichiro hit his first professional home run on June 12, 1993, off Hideo Nomo of the Kintetsu Buffaloes. Hideo is now with the Los Angeles Dodgers and was the 1995 National League Rookie of the Year.

from veteran manager Bobby Valentine, who had claimed that he was one of the top five players in the world. Even Ichiro wondered if he could compete at the next level: "Sometimes I am nervous, sometimes anxious, but I want to challenge a new world."

After the first month of the 2001 season, however, the question was no longer about Ichiro's ability to adapt to the big leagues, but whether major league players could adjust to *him*. "He's a legitimate hitter, no question," declared Yankees manager Joe Torre. "I don't think you can pitch him one way. You can go in and out, up and down; but he makes the adjustment. You can get ahead in the count, and Suzuki still seems relaxed. He doesn't seem to have any weaknesses."

In addition to his hitting ability, Ichiro also quickly showed that he was just as adept at stealing bases and playing right field. He had, in fact, sent shock waves through the American League when, in the second week of the season, he threw out Terrence Long, the Oakland A's fleet-footed center fielder, who had attempted to go from first to third on a single to right. "Ichiro may be the most fundamentally-sound outfielder in the game," noted Texas Rangers manager Buck Showalter. "He has a great clock in him.

"I cannot be the player I am without defense and speed. I may impress you with my hitting, but it's my defense and running that make me a good player."

He always knows just how much time is needed to make the play."

Ichiro finished the season even more spectacularly than he had started it, as he became the first player since Jackie Robinson to lead the majors in both batting average and stolen bases. In addition to setting a host of host of records, including most hits by a rookie, Ichiro also led the Mariners to a record-tying 116 victories. "He's the engine of our train," said Seattle center fielder Mike Cameron. "He's the one who makes us go."

He was the first rookie to win a batting title since Tony Oliva of the Minnesota Twins did it in 1964.

Ichiro, who was awarded a Gold Glove for fielding excellence, became just the second player to win both the Rookie of the Year and MVP awards in the same season. "Ichiro is unique," said Lou Piniella, who managed the Mariners during Ichiro's first two big league seasons. "You can't compare him with anybody."

"Don't you think that now kids think they can play in the big leagues because they see someone like me make it?" asked Ichiro, who is 5' 9" and weighs 160 pounds.

Although he had had one of the greatest rookie seasons ever, Ichiro approached the 2002 campaign without a backward glance. "Last year is gone," he said. "It's history. I just want to build on my experiences and hopefully have another great season."

Ichiro maximizes his potential with vigorous regimens, which involve not just his body, but his mind as well. "The goal is to have no regrets at the end of every day," he says. "It would be nice to be perfect on a daily basis, but since we're human beings, that's impossible. So the goal is to be as close as possible. In order to achieve that, it is imperative to set aside some self-reflection time each day."

MOST HITS EVER RECORDED BY A ROOKIE

Player	Team	Year	Hits
Ichiro Suzuki	Mariners	2001	242
Shoeless Joe Jackson	Cleveland	1911	233
Lloyd Waner	Pirates	1927	223
Tony Oliva	Twins	1964	217
Dale Alexander	Tigers	1929	215

Although a slump during the final two months of the season cut into his gaudy numbers, Ichiro still managed to finish among the American League leaders in hits, triples, batting average, stolen bases, runs, and on-base percentage. "I'm not a

> "He does something different every time he steps up to the plate," said Toronto Blue Jays pitcher, Roy Halladay.
> "He slaps, he has power, he hits the ball where it's pitched. And with his speed, you don't know what's going to happen."

machine," said Suzuki, whose 450 hits represent the most ever accumulated in the first two years of a career. "But I have learned from whatever happened at the end of last year."

He learned so well in fact, that he tore up A.L pitching for a .356 average during the first three months of the 2003 season, and led the Mariners to the best record in baseball. "I was a pitcher in high school," said Ichiro, breaking into a broad smile. "But if I had to pitch to *me* now, I don't think I could get this guy out."

Although he has recorded astonishing achievements throughout his baseball career, Ichiro has continued to march to his very own drummer. "Personally, I don't like the term *success*," he explained. "It's too arbitrary and relative. It's usually someone else's definition, not yours. Each person needs to learn to stay within himself, set his own personal goals and decide for himself what being a success really means. "I wanted to be the first player to show what Japanese batters can do in the major leagues," explained Ichiro. "I had a dream. And I made that dream come true."

CAREER STATS *

Hitting		Fielding	
AVERAGE	.337	TOTAL CHANCES	994
HITS	565	ASSTS	22
2B	76	ERRORS	5
3B	19	PERCENTAGE	.994
HR	23		
RUNS	297		
RBI	146		
SB	108		

*As of June 30, 2003

Alfonso Soriano

Alfonso Soriano

Although Alfonso Soriano has had to overcome a great many obstacles in order to achieve his success, he's always maintained a positive approach to the game. "I've always believed in myself, and I was always willing to work hard to achieve my goals. That's all I want to do, all the time, get better and better."

> "Every time I walk out onto the field, I feel that I can be the best one in the game, and that I can be a superstar."

Soriano was born January 7, 1978 and was raised by his mother, Andrea, in San Pedro de Macoris, in the Dominican Republic, a small island country that has produced an amazing number of major league superstars, including right-fielders Sammy Sosa and Vladimir Guerrero, and shortstop Miguel Tejada.

Early on, however, it didn't see likely that the young shortstop would ever get a chance to play baseball for a living. While he watched many of his friends and his two older brothers sign minor league contracts,

> When Soriano was growing up, he was nicknamed "The Mule," because he was a slow runner.

Soriano had been totally ignored by major league scouts. Even his uncle and former minor leaguer Hilario, who is now a scouting supervisor for the Toronto Blue Jays, didn't think his nephew had the skills to become a big league ballplayer.

So when he turned 16 in 1994, Soriano simply accepted the only offer he had received and signed with the Hiroshima Toyo Carp of the Japanese Central League. After spending the next two years working out at the team's baseball academy in the Dominican Republic, he finally took the 15-hour flight to Japan to play for the Carp's minor league team during the 1996 season.

He quickly found out that Japanese teams have rigid training techniques; players were compelled to practice from eight in the morning until after dark. "I thought about quitting every day. It was so bad, that the first time I came home from Japan, my mother saw my hands and said, `You're not going back,'" recalled Soriano, who had also struggled with homesickness and the difficulties of learning a new language. "I had blisters all over my hands from hitting so

"I am grateful for my experience in Japan, the Carp made me a better player."

much. I had never hit like that. Hitting in the cold, against pitching machines, it was unbelievable. But I went back because I loved baseball, and once I was there I could dedicate myself and keep my mind positive."

After two relatively unproductive seasons in Japan, Soriano took the advice of his former agent, Don Nomura, and decided to try to get a major league team to sign him. Due to an agreement between Japan and Major League Baseball, however, Soriano was

forced to sit out the 1998 season. In the meantime, he worked out in Los Angeles every day and played in a recreational league on weekends.

"It was difficult," said Soriano. "Don was sure it would work out, but I was getting frustrated and desperate. I had never gone eight months before without playing—every time I struck out against some old guy, I was sure no one would ever want to sign me."

Despite his concerns, Soriano wound up working out for eight teams, and made a strong impression on most of them. "I knew he hadn't played against good competition recently, but there wasn't any rust on him," says Dave Wilder, who was the Cubs' farm director at the time. "But he was banging ball after ball into the street, and the crack of his bat made everyone stop and ask who he was."

But the New York Yankees wound up outbidding all of the other the teams, inking Soriano to a four-year, $3.1 million deal. During the next two years, he rose rapidly through the Yankees' farm system, and was quickly identified as one of the top prospects in the minors. "While he was playing in Double A, people were saying he was just like a young Vladimir Guerrero," recalled Yankee general manager Brian Cashman, in comparing Soriano to the Montreal Expos' slugger, whom many consider to be the best all-around player in the game. "Our scouts were telling me that someday he would hit 30 home runs and be a major offensive player at his position."

Despite, and partially due to, his potential, Soriano had become trade-bait for the Yankees, who were set at the shortstop position with their team-leader, Derek Jeter. In fact, the Yankees had agreed to send Soriano to the Houston Astros for outfielder Moises

"One of the things I like about him is that he doesn't crawl into a shell," said Yankees manager Joe Torre. " He's tough. He's not afraid. He doesn't back off — he's very aggressive."

Alou in the spring of 2000, but Alou, who had right of approval, vetoed the deal. "Sometimes," noted Yankees coach, Lee Mazzilli, "the best trades are the ones you *don't* make."

Although the Yankees had invited Soriano to spring training in 2001, he had been expected to spend the season with their Triple A team in the International League. But his tremendous hitting and athleticism caused the team to quickly reconsider their plans. "His offense is good enough to carry any position, and he proved that he could play left field," said Cashman. "Within a week, it was clear to us that he was our best defensive outfielder."

Before spring training ended, however, Soriano had been switched to second base, and forced to learn a new position on the fly. "It's going to take awhile," cautioned Derek Jeter. "Anytime you play on one side

"If I make a mistake here and there, I'm going to come back and try to play even more aggressive. That's how I play the game."

of the infield your whole career and then

switch to the other, balls come off the bat a different way. You're used to seeing runners when you turn a double play, and now you don't know where they are."

But Soriano had been able to make the transition and survive the anxiety of playing for a championship team that was trying to win its fourth straight World Series, and to do it in the bright glare of Yankee Stadium, where excellence is expected. Although he did have predictable problems in the field, Soriano excelled in every other facet of the game, as he batted .278, smacked 18 home runs, collected 78 RBI and swiped 43 bases. "It was very difficult, but when you're working hard, you can make anything happen," said Soriano, who finished third in the vot-

"He has special talent. He can become a great second baseman," said Joe Morgan, television analyst and Hall of Fame second baseman. "In fact, he just may become the best one ever."

ing for the Rookie of the Year award. "I convinced myself that I can do everything, play in New York and play a new position. When I have my mind set like that, *anything* is possible."

Then he'd proceeded to shine even brighter in postseason play, as he hit a game-ending homer in Game 4 of the ALCS against the Seattle Mariners and smacked a single to win Game 5 of the World Series against the Arizona Diamondbacks. Then, he golfed a towering go-ahead home run in the eighth inning of

Game 7, which would have stood as one of the greatest moments in the team's storied history, if the Diamondbacks hadn't rallied to win an inning later. "When you do what he did, when you hit a home run in the seventh game of the World Series, well, that's a pretty good commentary on where you fit on *our* club," said manager Joe Torre. "He feels like he belongs."

"His package of power, speed and makeup is unique," said teammate Roger Clemens. "He'll take your nastiest pitch and hurt it bad. I call him Senor Peligroso: Mr. Dangerous."

"As I was rounding the bases I was thinking about my family who was watching the game back in the Dominican Republic. I knew they could not be here with me, but I was hoping they were watching it on television and enjoying it."

After Soriano had torn up the Grapefruit League the following spring, Torre rewarded his performance by moving him into the leadoff spot in the batting order. And Soriano had responded by leading the American League in hits, runs and stolen bases, while slugging 39 home runs, a league record by a second baseman. Soriano added to his reputation by slugging a Big Fly in the 2002 All-Star Game, and earning the Silver Slugger Award as the top-hitting second baseman in the A.L. "I won't tell you

what his ceiling is," said Yankee hitting coach Rick Downs. "Because in a year or two, it might become his floor."

Soriano finished third in the voting for the 2002 MVP award and has continued to bang the ball in 2003, ranking among the A.L leaders in hits, runs, stolen bases and home runs. "I'm working hard because I want to be perfect," explains Soriano, who is the leading vote getter for the All-Star game. "I know I'm never going to reach that goal, but I'll keep working toward it every day."

CAREER STATS *			
Hitting		Fielding	
AVERAGE	.283	TOTAL CHANCES	1,857
HITS	479	ERRORS	60
2B	100	PERCENTAGE	.968
3B	8		
HR	81		
RUNS	280		
RBI	227		
SB	110		

*As of June 30, 2003

Michael Vick

Michael Vick

"Once I decided football was the way for me, there was no looking back," explained Michael Vick. "*Nothing was going to distract me.*"

Vick was born June 26, 1980, and raised in the Ridley Circle neighborhood of Newport News, Virginia, where drugs and violence have done in too many young men. "Sports kept me off the streets. It kept me from getting into all the bad stuff that was going on," added Vick, who credits the Hampton Roads Boys and Girls Club for giving the neighborhood children a safe environment in which to gather and learn various skills. "That was where we started our football careers, and it led a lot of us to go on to play high school and college ball," said Vick, who has since become one of the Boys and Girls Club's biggest supporters.

> "I like the way he's developed," said Vick's father, Michael Boddie, "not only as a player but also as a person."

Vick's ability to throw a football immediately caught the eye of Warwick High School's football coach, Tommy Reamon, a former NFL running back. "He was only in ninth grade when I first saw him zip the ball with that quick release, and I said, '*Wow!*'

Although Reamon had been beguiled by Vick's potential, he decided to start him off on the junior varsity squad, allowing Vick to grow his game against players that were his own age. But after the strong-armed prodigy threw for 20 touchdown passes in just six games, Reamon installed Vick as the team's starting quarterback. And the left-handed throwing freshman quickly validated his coach's decision by throwing for 433 yards in only his second start with the varsity.

During his four years at Warwick, Vick developed into a top-tier college prospect, but there wasn't anyone in the area who thought that he would go on to become a superstar. "I think people would be lying if they told you they knew he would be the type of player he is today," declared Bill Dee, who had coached against Vick-led teams. "It's easy to look smart now, but back then we didn't know if Michael was a diamond in the rough, or just another piece of pretty glass."

Vick, in fact, wasn't even considered the best quarterback in his area, an honor that was reserved for Ronald Curry, who went on to have an uneven career at North Carolina, and who has thrown only one pass for the Oakland Raiders. "I lived in his shadow," recalled Vick. "At the end of my senior year, I ended up sec-o-n-d-t-e-a-m everything. Being second was something I had to deal with, and deal with a lot."

Vick, however, began to show that he was in a class of his own in his very first college game, when he led Virginia Tech to an opening day victory and scored a trio of touchdowns, including a head-over-heels touchdown leap that made highlight reels all across the nation. The 19-year-old continued to sparkle throughout the remainder of the fall, as he posted the second-best passer-efficiency rating in NCAA history, leading the Hokies to their first undefeated season, and a National Championship match-up against the heavily favored and No.1-rated Florida State Seminoles. Although FSU was able to survive an amazing Vick-led rally that had staked VT into a 29-28 lead, it was the fabulous first-year player who had won most of the applause. "Michael Vick is probably the best quarterback in America," said Syracuse coach Paul Pasqualoni. "There's not a team at any level that's got an answer for him."

"I know most people didn't think we belonged on the same field as FSU and that the freshman quarterback would choke," said Vick, whose legs and arm had accounted for 322 of Tech's 503 total yards against the nation's best defense. "But those people didn't know me. I love competition. I love a challenge, and I don't back down

from *anything*. We took it to the 'Noles, and at one point I asked those guys, 'Do y'all think we're here for *nothing?*'"

Despite the fact that he had been somewhat hampered by an injury in his second season at the helm of the Hokies, Vick still managed to lead the team to a lopsided Gator Bowl win over Clemson and another

> "After the Sugar Bowl Game against FSU, I pretty much realized that things would never be the same for me ever again."

top-ten national ranking. Then Vick, who had compiled a 20-1 record as a two-year starter, while establishing himself as the premiere quarterback in the college ranks, decided to test himself at the next level and entered the 2001 NFL draft.

Although it wasn't a stretch to claim that Vick might have been the best athlete ever to have played quarterback in college, many scouts and coaches thought that he should have spent another season at Tech developing his passing skills and techniques. Television analyst and former NFL coach Mike Ditka, however, wasn't concerned. "He's going to be one of the great ones in the NFL," declared Ditka. "If I had any picks, I'd give them all up for the next couple of years just to get him."

Atlanta head coach Dan Reeves thought so highly of Vick's pro prospects that he engineered a trade with the San Diego Chargers that allowed the Falcons to select the young quarterback with the first overall pick in the 2002 draft. Vick's preseason practices quickly showed the Falcons that they had received even more than they had hoped for. "I had no idea that he was

such a hard worker, a true team player, and a deep-down competitor," said Jack Burns, the Falcons former quarterbacks coach. "I knew he had a strong arm, but it's stronger than I realized, and his accuracy is much better than I thought it would be. He's also shown a fine ability to read defenses under pressure, which is exceptional for a guy his age who doesn't have a lot of experience in pocket-passing."

Reeves had chosen to bring Vick along slowly in 2001, using him in special situations, and when veteran signal caller Chris Chandler was injured. That first season proved to be a mixed bag for Vick, who suffered through the normal growing pains of an NFL initiation. "I'd always come in and do some good things," recalled Vick, "but there'd always be something that set me back. Whether it was a sack or a fumble, something would go wrong and it was like a smack in the face."

In a late-season game in Miami, though, Vick gave the league a taste of what was to come when he connected on two long passes and racked up more than 50 yards on the ground. "He's the best athlete in the NFL," declared Dolphins cornerback

> "Vick's the real deal," said TV analyst John Madden. "He's so exciting, and it seems like every time he gets his hands on the football, he can take it to the house and score. I've never seen anyone like him."

Patrick Surtain. "It doesn't always matter how well you defend one of their receivers, because his arm is so good, he can throw the ball right past you."

"I think he's as ready as any second-year quarterback can be in this league," said Falcons coach Dan Reeves, after he'd named Vick the starter for the 2002 season. "I know he's not going to do everything right, but we think he's going to make a lot of good decisions." Then Vick went out and confirmed his coach's confidence by unexpectedly leading the Falcons into the playoffs, and earning Pro Bowl honors for himself.

With an ability to throw the ball 80 yards and the speed to outrun defensive backs, Vick is threatening to revolutionize the quarterback position. "The NFL has never seen the kind of speed and athleticism that Michael Vick brings," declared Hall of Fame defensive end Lee Roy Selmon. "What he is doing to the game with his arm and legs is unprecedented."

"He has the whole package wrapped up in one body," said Philadelphia Eagles defensive tackle Corey Simon. "And it can be very scary if you're on the outside looking in."

But what has defensive coordinators around the league staying up late at night is the realization that in terms of experience, Vick is still a toddler in the NFL. "The more years I get under my belt, the more I age, the better I become," he said matter-of-factly. "I trust it and know it, and I can see it coming."

"He's one of the most talented players to ever play the game," said Green Bay Packers quarterback Brett Favre. "He strikes terror into opposing teams, and there aren't many players who are able to do that."

CAREER STATS *

Passing		Rushing	
ATTEMPTS	534	ATTEMPTS	144
COMPLETIONS	281	YARDS	1,066
PERCENTAGE	52.6	AVERAGE	7.4
YARDS	3,721	TOUCHDOWNS	9
TOUCHDOWNS	18		
INTERCEPTIONS	11		
QB RATING	77.6		

Vick was the youngest quarterback to start in the NFL during the 2002 season, and only the sixth since 1970 to be voted into the Pro Bowl in his first year at the helm.

With a total of 1,066 rushing yards, Vick has run for more yards in his first two seasons than any other quarterback in league history.

Kobe Bryant

Kobe Bryant

Kobe Bryant has always maintained that in order for people to soar toward their dreams, they must believe in themselves, work hard and keep moving forward to achieve their aims.

"As a kid I wanted to be a basketball player, and nothing was going to stop me from reaching my goal," explained Bryant. "I used to go to basketball camps, where they would tell me that only one out of every million players make it to the pros. I just told myself, *'That's me. I'm that one.'* That's the type of determination I feel is needed."

> **"Seven rings, eight rings, nine rings, I don't care," explained Bryant. "I just want to win. Every year."**

Bryant, who was born August 23, 1978 in Philadelphia, Pennsylvania, had started to display that attitude as a young boy. "I've been like this since I was five," said Bryant, who first became interested in basketball through his dad, Joe "Jelly Bean" Bryant, who had been an NBA journeyman for the first half of his 16-year career and a European player for the latter half. "My passion started when I was a little kid, playing basketball with my father, wanting to be like Dad."

When Bryant was six, the family moved to Italy, when his father signed with an Italian team. "It was difficult at first, because I couldn't speak the language," recalled Bryant, who is currently part-owner of a team in Italy. "But my older sisters and I got together after school to teach each other new words. Within a few months, I was able to speak Italian pretty well."

Bryant also learned to play basketball, partly by watching his dad play, but also by studying tapes of NBA greats, and then going out and mimicking their moves. "I was like a computer," recalled Bryant. "I would watch everybody, from Magic Johnson to Michael Jordan. I'd copy their pet moves and add them to my game. I was always looking for ways to get better."

> "I don't know what the big deal is about playing on the road. I've never seen fans scream loud enough to block my jump shot."

During the family's eight-year stay in Europe, Bryant also learned the basic skills of basketball from Italian coaches. "In Italy, they teach you the ABCs of basketball," explained Bryant, who returned to America in time to attend Lower Merion High School, outside of Philadelphia. "When I came back to the states, and saw everybody dunking and doing fancy things, I just figured I'd pick up those skills. If you have the fundamentals down at an early age, you can advance much quicker."

Bryant's play caught the eye of Lower Merion coach Gregg Downer at the team's very first practice. "I knew right away I had something unbelievable, something special," Downer said. "He was 6' 2" and 140 pounds. Physically, he wasn't very mature, but there was a fundamental foundation to his play. After five minutes, I turned to

somebody and said, `That kid's a pro.'"

Which is exactly what Bryant must have looked like to opposing players after a junior year in which he averaged 31.1 points, 10.4 rebounds and 5.2 assists and was named the 1995 Pennsylvania Player of the Year. Bryant's play had brought scores of college coaches and scouts to Lower Merion, and created something of a circus atmosphere at their home games. "It was overwhelming," recalled Downer. "The only one who never seemed flustered by it was Kobe. He just kept cool and played even harder."

The following year, Bryant led the Aces to their first title in 42 years, and was named the National High School Player of the Year by a raft of organizations and publications, including *USA TODAY* and *Parade* magazine. And for the first time in his life, Bryant was finally able to out-play

> "I'm out there playing my butt off every single night," declared Bryant. "I love it so much that I play every minute like it's my last."

his dad in their one-on-one games. "I had to make up certain rules," recalled a smiling Joe Bryant. "We only played a low-post game, and I refereed and kept score. Even if Kobe hit five baskets in a row, when he'd ask me the score, I'd tell him, 'I'm up one. Dad's *always* up one.'"

After the season ended, Bryant, who broke the four-decade old Southeastern Pennsylvania career scoring record established by Hall of Famer Wilt

Chamberlain, announced that he was going to enter the 1996 NBA draft. "I didn't know if I could play in this league, but I had a lot of confidence," said Bryant, who had regularly competed against college and NBA players in the Philadelphia area. "I knew that if I began to struggle, I'd just work harder."

Jerry West, the former vice president of the Los Angeles Lakers, had been so taken by Bryant's attitude and potential, that he traded Vlade Divac, LA's starting center, to the Charlotte Hornets in order to acquire the rights to Bryant, who had been picked up by Charlotte with the 13th overall selection. "He just blew us away when we brought him for a workout," recalled West, one of the greatest backcourt players of all. "We had never seen *anyone* do the things he did."

"He has an uncommon will to win," said San Antonio Spurs coach Gregg Popovich. "It's the exact same will that Michael Jordan had."

After the draft, Bryant impressed the Lakers staff by collecting tapes of all the league's other shooting guards, so he could watch and learn their strengths and weaknesses.

Although Bryant received only scant playing time during his initial season with a veteran Lakers team, he lit up All-Star Weekend when he soared to the Slam Dunk title and scored a record 31 points in the Rookie Game. The following year, the Lakers had used Bryant as their sixth man, but his high-wire creativity had thrilled so many fans, that they voted him into the starting lineup for the 1998 All-Star Game. The league tried to portray that game as a passing of the torch, from Michael Jordan, who is generally considered to be the greatest player of all time, to Bryant, who many thought would take Jordan's place as the game's premiere performer. But Bryant, who became the youngest player to start in an All-Star Game, didn't buy into the hype. "I don't want to be the next Michael Jordan. I just want to be the best player that I can be."

"I see a lot of myself in him," said Michael Jordan. "No doubt about it."

Bryant maximizes his talents by working harder than any other NBA player during the offseason, usually spending eight hours a day in the gym. "It was like he was put on earth to be a great basketball player, and everything he does is dedicated to becoming that," noted Lakers guard Brian Shaw, who has known Bryant since he was nine-years-old. "The only guy I've been around with that kind of work ethic is Larry Bird."

Bryant became a starter at the beginning of the 1998-1999 season and quickly established himself as one of the most exciting players in the league. With an explosive first step and the ability to slash to the hoop and elevate over seven-foot centers, Bryant became one of the

most feared scorers in the league. "Nobody can guard Kobe one-on-one," said former LA coach Del Harris. "*Nobody.*"

> **"I'm playing against the greatest players in the world. The competition—that's what I've always wanted."**

Bryant has continued to put in the work, and his game has improved each year since he's been in the league. Instead of merely using his athleticism to take it to the rim, Bryant has developed into a complete package, one who can post-up an opponent as easily as he can deflate a team with his jump shot. During the previous season, in fact, he canned an NBA-record 12 3-pointers against the Seattle Supersonics, including an unprecedented nine in a row during one stretch. It was the start of an amazing run in which he scored 35-plus points in 13 straight games, including nine in a row when he topped the 40 mark. "My hand was in his face; *my momma's hand was in his face,*" complained Bonzi Wells after Bryant

had torched the Portland TrailBlazers. "We have good defenders, but he made us look like no *defenders.*"

Bryant, who helped lead the Lakers to three consecutive NBA titles from 2000—2002, has become such a complete player that he was named to the All-NBA First Team, and the All-Defensive First Team in 2003.

> **"Taking a shot with the game on the line, that's what I live for."**

"What I'm doing right now, I'm chasing perfection," explained Bryant, who finished second in the league in scoring and third in the voting for MVP. " And if I don't get it, I'm going to get *this* close."

NBA PER GAME CAREER STATS	
POINTS	21.5
F.G. PERCENTAGE	559
REBOUNDS	5.0
ASSISTS	4.2
STEALS	1.44

In 2003, the 24-year-old Bryant posted career highs in scoring average (30), assists (5.9) and rebounds (6.9).

On March 5, 2003, Bryant became the youngest player ever to reach the 10,000-point milestone.

Yao Ming

Yao Ming

Although giants are usually thought of as awkward and clumsy, the 7' 5" Yao Ming displays the grace of a dancer and the soul of a poet.

"Every sound in the gym is so fantastic—the screams of the fans, the whistle of the ref, the clamor of teammates calling to each other, the bang of the ball bouncing off the boards, the squeaking sound of sneakers rubbing against the wooden floor. I just love those sounds of competition: the muscle, the sweat and the sound of the ball swishing through the net."

> "I play the game in two parts. One part is the enjoyment of playing. The other part, of course, is winning."

Yao Ming was born September 12, 1980 and raised in Shanghai, the largest city in China, which is home to more than eleven million people. Yao had been introduced to basketball by his mother, Fang Feng Di, who is 6' 3", and his father, Yao Zhi Yuan, who stands at 6' 7". Both of his parents had been accomplished hoopsters and had played for China's National Teams.

Despite his size, Yao was initially tentative about playing basketball. He had grown so quickly early in his life that his body had become uncoordinated, and although he towered over other boys his age, he lacked the strength and stamina to keep up with his shorter teammates. When he was nine, however, his parents enrolled him in sports school, and by the time he was 14 Yao had become so skilled that he was selected to play for the Shanghai Youth Team. Three years later, Yao turned professional and averaged 10 points and 8.3 rebounds during the 1997-1998 season with the Shanghai Sharks of the China Basketball Association. Yao's abilities grew in each succeeding season with the Sharks, and he emerged as the preeminent player in China during the 2000-2001 season, averaging 19.4 rebounds, 5.5 blocked shots and 27.1 points per game. Yao asserted his dominance the following year as well, when he averaged a career-high 32.4 points, while shooting an amazing .721 from the field, and led the Sharks to their first CBA Championship. In the final round against the Bayi Rockets, Yao brought his game to an even higher level, averaging 41.3 points, 21 rebounds and 4.3 blocks. Then he sealed the deal in the clinching 123-122 victory by scoring 44 points on 21-of-21 shooting, with 21 rebounds and seven blocked shots.

He was the league MVP in each of his final two seasons in the CBA.

Yao averaged 23.4 points on .651 shooting, and 15.4 rebounds in his 122 games with the Shanghai Sharks of the China Basketball Association.

Yao's size and achievements in the CBA and as a member of Chinese National Team made him one of the most intriguing players in the world, and the Houston Rockets decided to tap into his vast potential when they made him the No. 1 pick in the 2002 NBA draft. Although the league had already opened its doors to more than 50 international players,

including fellow Chinese National Team members Wang Zhizhi and Mengke Bateer, Yao became the first and only number one pick to come from an international basketball league.

Yao, who had wanted to play in the most competitive basketball league in the world, surprised some of the NBA's top talent when the Chinese National Team came to Indianapolis to compete in the World Basketball Championship during the summer of 2002. "He's got a nice shooting touch, and he has great court awareness and passing ability," said Detroit Piston star Ben Wallace, the NBA's 2002 and 2003 Defensive Player of the Year. "He'll need to get stronger in his upper body, but once he does that and gains some experience, he'll be a real factor in the league."

Because contract problems had caused him to miss training camp and all but two exhibition games, Yao got off to a slow start in the 2002-2003 season. But in the sixth game, he tossed in 20 points in just 23 minutes against the defending champion Los Angeles Lakers, and two games later, threw down 30 points and grabbed 16 boards in 33 minutes of action against the Dallas Mavericks in a nationally-televised game. "With his size and skills," said TV analyst and Hall of Fame center

Bill Walton, "Yao has a chance to alter the way the game of basketball is played."

"He has all the tools," said Lakers center Shaquille O'Neal. "He can shoot. He can dribble. He's no slouch."

Yao's friendly and humble personality had also created a positive impact among basketball fans around the world, who chose him ahead of Shaquille O'Neal as the Western Conference All-Star squad's starting center. Yao's demeanor and work ethic also had an immediate impact upon his Rocket teammates, who nicknamed him 'Dynasty'. "Yao is one great dude," said guard Cuttino Mobley. "Modest, not cocky; always hugging us, always wanting to learn."

"The guy can play," said New Orleans Hornets point guard Baron Davis. " And I like him a lot."

Despite the fact that he had missed all of training camp, was saddled with the demands of a frenzied media, and encumbered by the pressures of adapting to a new culture and language, Yao maintained his composure and his presence. "I did not think I would play that well this season," said Yao, who was a unanimous selection to the NBA All-Rookie First Team and finished second behind Phoenix Suns power forward Amare Stoudemire in the voting for the Rookie of the Year Award. "Now that I've gained experience and can work on my training, I expect to do better next season."

After the season, Yao went home to China and hosted a telethon to help raise money for the fight against SARS, a disease that has spread panic throughout the world. "Everyone needs to contribute to the good of the world," said Yao.

Most NBA officials agree that Yao will continue to improve, and many of the top talent evaluators in the league expect a whole lot more. "It may take him one or two years to acclimate himself and to get to where he understands his position in the NBA, said Indiana Pacers president Donnie Walsh. "But I think he'll be great player in this league for a long time."

NBA PER GAME CAREER STATS	
POINTS	13.5
F.G. PERCENTAGE	.498
REBOUNDS	8.2
ASSISTS	1.7
BLOCKS	1.7

ORDER FORM

If you enjoyed this book, you might want to order some of the other exciting titles written by Richard J. Brenner, the best-selling sportswriter in America.

Quantiy

BOUND FOR GLORY: Includes full-color photos and biographical sketches of Michael Vick, Alfonso Soriano, Ichiro Suzuki, Yao Ming and Kobe Bryant. 32 pages. ($4.99/$6.99 Can.) _____

FOOTBALL SUPERSTARS ALBUM 2002: Includes 16 full-color pages of the game's top players, plus bios and career stats. 48 pages. ($4.99/$6.99 Can.) _____

KURT WARNER* PEYTON MANNING A dual biography of two of football's top quarterbacks. 96 pages, including 12 full-color pages. ($4.50/$6.50 Can.) _____

BRETT FAVRE: An easy-to-read, full-color, photo-filled biography especially for younger readers. 32 pages. ($4.50/$6.50 Can.) _____

DEREK JETER: An easy-to-read, full-color, photo-filled biography especially for younger readers. 32 pages. ($4.50/$6.50 Can.) _____

SAMMY SOSA: An easy-to-read, full-color, photo-filled biography especially for younger readers. 32 pages. ($4.50/$6.50 Can.) _____

MARK MCGWIRE: An easy-to-read, full-color, photo-filled biography especially for younger readers. 32 pages. ($4.50/$6.50 Can.) _____

KOBE BRYANT: An easy-to-read, full-color, photo-filled biography especially for younger readers. 32 pages. ($3.95/$5.95 Can.) _____

SUPER SPORTS STARS BOOK OF RECORDS (1999): by Bob Carroll and Pete Palmer. Career, game, and season records for baseball, basketball, football and hockey. 64 pages. ($3.99/$5.99 Can.) _____

TOTAL NUMBER OF BOOKS ORDERED _____

TOTAL COST OF BOOKS _____

TAX (*NY State residents must add appropriate sales tax.*) _____

POSTAGE and HANDLING CHARGES _____
(*$1.75 per book, up to a maximum of $10.50; ($2.00, up to a maximum of $12.00 in Canada)*)

TOTAL PAYMENT ENCLOSED (*Credit cards not accepted. All payments must be in U.S. currency.*) _____

NAME_____

STREET ADDRESS_____

CITY_____ STATE_____ ZIP CODE_____ COUNTRY_____

SEND PAYMENT TO: EAST END PUBLISHING, 54 ALEXANDER DR., SYOSSET, NY 11791

Discounts are available on orders of 25 or more books.

For details, write or call (516) 364-6383, or e-mail us at rbrenne2@optonline.net